The Bell in the Well

Jeanne Willis
Illustrated by Francesca Carabelli

Rigby
A Harcourt Achieve Imprint

www.Rigby.com
1-800-531-5015

Jill lived in a cottage
with her stepmother, Nasty Nell.

One day, it was about to rain
when Nell yelled, "Hang out the
laundry, Jill!"

"I want it dry by three o'clock!"

Nasty Nell gave Jill impossible jobs such as this all the time.

Jill hung out the laundry
and the rain began to fall.

"This will never dry by three!"
she cried, "Whatever shall I do?"

"Ring my bell!"
sang the wishing well.

There was a bell
in the bucket of the wishing well.

Jill rang it and wished for sunshine.
Suddenly, the sun began to shine.
Jill slipped the bell
into her pocket to keep it safe.

By three o'clock,
the laundry was dry.

"How did she do that?"
thought Nasty Nell.

Nasty Nell sent Jill to get firewood.
"Fill three sacks!" she yelled.

It was impossible.
The fog was too thick.

Jill rang the bell.
The sun shone, the fog lifted,
and Jill filled three sacks.

"How did she do that?"
thought Nasty Nell.

Nasty Nell sent Jill
to pick some berries.

"Fill three baskets!" she yelled.

It was impossible.
The berries were covered
in thick snow.

This time, Nasty Nell followed Jill.
Nell saw Jill shake the bell
and wish for sunshine.

The sun shone, the snow thawed,
and Jill filled three baskets.

"*That's* how she does it!"
thought Nell.

That night, Nasty Nell
stole the bell
from Jill's pocket.

In the morning, she sent
Jill to catch fish
during a big storm.

"Catch three fish!" she yelled.

Impossible!
The storm grew worse.
Jill reached for the bell,
but it was gone!

Crash! A huge wave
washed Jill out to sea.

The storm grew worse and worse.

Nasty Nell's cottage
was under water.

14

Her bed and bathtub floated away.

She climbed onto the roof
with the magic bell.

Nasty Nell rang the bell
and wished for sunshine.

She shook it and shook it,
but the sun would not shine.

The storm only grew worse.

She shook the bell so hard,
she dropped it.

Splash! It fell into the water.

A bird grabbed the bell
and took it to Jill.

Jill rang the bell
and wished for sunshine.

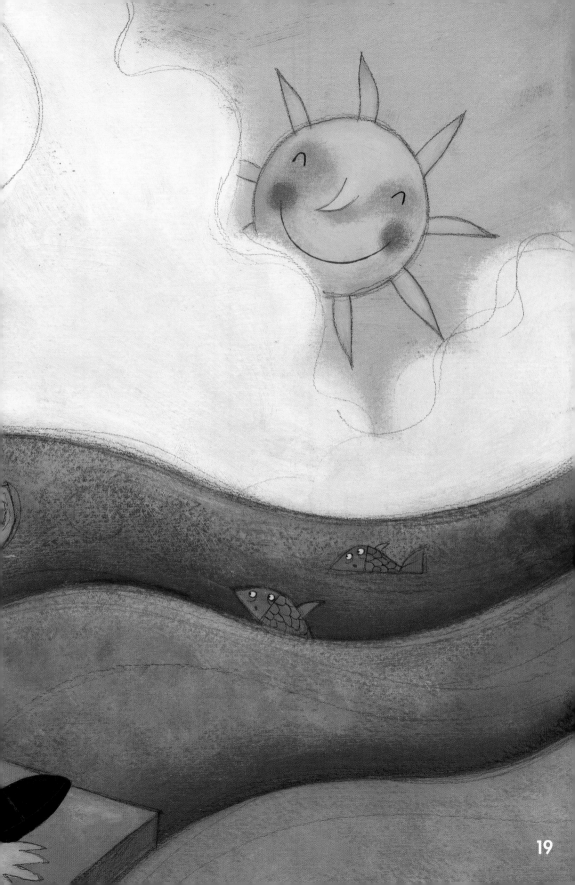

The sun shone, the storm stopped.

Jill floated to the shore.

There she met three lovely sisters.

"Come and play with us!"
said Milly, Tilly, and Lilly.

The three sisters had a mother named Jolly Molly.

Jill told Jolly Molly all about Nasty Nell.

Jolly Molly invited Jill to stay and live with them.

From that day on, every day felt like a sunny day.

And the girls danced and played.

Around and around we go,
As the wind gently blows.
Our friendship grows and grows
Beneath the sun's warm glow.